BEYOND THE BATTLEFIELD

Journalists

ALLEN R. WELLS

Rourke
Educational Media

A Division of
Carson
Dellosa
Education

Before Reading: *Building Background Knowledge and Vocabulary*

Building background knowledge can help children process new information and build upon what they already know. Before reading a book, it is important to tap into what children already know about the topic. This will help them develop their vocabulary and increase their reading comprehension.

Questions and Activities to Build Background Knowledge:

1. Look at the front cover of the book and read the title. What do you think this book will be about?
2. What do you already know about this topic?
3. Take a book walk and skim the pages. Look at the table of contents, photographs, captions, and bold words. Did these text features give you any information or predictions about what you will read in this book?

Vocabulary: *Vocabulary Is Key to Reading Comprehension*

Use the following directions to prompt a conversation about each word.

- Read the vocabulary words.
- What comes to mind when you see each word?
- What do you think each word means?

Vocabulary Words:
- censored
- concentration camp
- front lines
- photojournalist
- propaganda
- reporter

During Reading: *Reading for Meaning and Understanding*

To achieve deep comprehension of a book, children are encouraged to use close reading strategies. During reading, it is important to have children stop and make connections. These connections result in deeper analysis and understanding of a book.

 Close Reading a Text

During reading, have children stop and talk about the following:

- Any confusing parts
- Any unknown words
- Text to text, text to self, text to world connections
- The main idea in each chapter or heading

Encourage children to use context clues to determine the meaning of any unknown words. These strategies will help children learn to analyze the text more thoroughly as they read.

When you are finished reading this book, turn to the next-to-last page for **After-Reading Questions** and an **Activity**.

Table of Contents

REPORTERS

Sir Basil Clarke

Sir Basil Clarke was a **reporter** at the Daily Mail in England during World War I. In October 1914, Clarke was sent to Belgium. The German Army was advancing on the city of Ostend, and the paper wanted Clarke there before the Germans arrived.

reporter (ri-POR-tur): someone who gathers and reports the news for a newspaper, magazine, or website

front lines (fruhnt linez): the military lines or parts of an army that are closest to the enemy

But he was too late. Journalists were not allowed at the **front lines** of war at the time, so Clarke was supposed to return home to London. Instead of going home, Clarke hid on a train full of French soldiers to get to the front lines in Dunkirk.

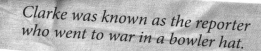

Clarke was known as the reporter who went to war in a bowler hat.

In Dunkirk, Clarke lived as a fugitive. He was exposed to the realities of the war up close. He interviewed soldiers, reported on what he saw, and sent the stories back to England. The British public was shocked by his reports. He was able to give the public the truth, and the truth was horrifying.

Clarke was finally forced to return home after being found out by local authorities. After the war, Clarke left his career as a journalist, but he is remembered for changing the way reporters cover war.

British soldiers in a battlefield trench during WWI, seen here during a break in fighting.

Marguerite Higgins

Marguerite Higgins became a reporter in 1942. Higgins's reporting was mostly focused on wars, beginning with the end of World War II. In 1944, American troops were about to liberate the **concentration camp** Dachau. Higgins beat them there, making her and a colleague the first Americans to arrive at Dachau.

Dachau

Dachau was the first Nazi concentration camp. It was used as the model for all concentration camps in Germany.

Marguerite Higgins

The concentration camp Dachau

concentration camp (kahn-suhn-TREY-shuhn kamp): a place where a large number of people (prisoners of war, refugees, or the members of an ethnic or religious group) are imprisoned under armed guard

Higgins continued her war reporting when the Korean War began in 1950. She wrote articles about her experiences on the front line. When female reporters were eventually banned from the front lines, Higgins got permission from a general she had previously interviewed to continue her work. Her boss threatened to fire her if she didn't come home, but Higgins knew her reporting was too important.

Because of her incredible reporting on the Korean War, Higgins received the Pulitzer Prize for International Reporting in 1951. She remained a writer for the rest of her life.

37 USA

Marguerite Higgins

2002

Vincent Lushington "Roi" Ottley

Vincent Lushington "Roi" Ottley was sent from the United States to Europe to report on the American armed forces during WWII. He was the first Black reporter hired by a major newspaper to cover the war.

Hypocrisy in America

Ottley was interested in the relationship between Black Americans struggling for civil rights at home while they fought for freedom in Europe. While reporting during WWII, he overheard a Black soldier say, "I'm going to get some of that Freedom they are talking about when I get home."

Ottley was already a well-known writer for his book, *New World A-Coming: Inside Black America.* This book highlighted the racial hypocrisy of America. While Americans were fighting a war for freedom in Europe, Black Americans didn't have equal freedoms at home.

Vincent Lushington "Roi" Ottley

Ottley wrote about race relations between American troops. He had to be careful about what he was writing. He often had to soften the realities of the relationships between Black and white troops to make sure he wasn't **censored**.

Ottely wanted to show the worth of Black people in the military. He dedicated a great number of his articles to the accomplishments of Black troops. He is remembered as a journalism pioneer for Black Americans.

Hometowns honor their returning veterans, 1945

censored (SEN-surd): to have removed parts of a writing, movie, or other work because it was thought of as offensive or unacceptable

PHOTOJOURNALISTS
Robert Capa

Robert Capa has been called one of the greatest photographers of the 20th century. Capa was born in Hungary but eventually immigrated to the U.S. He became a well-known **photojournalist** during the Spanish Civil War.

A Famous Fake?

Years after Capa's "The Falling Soldier" became famous, one journalist claimed that Capa told him the picture was staged. This claim was never proven, and the picture is still widely believed to be genuine.

The photograph that brought Capa fame was named "The Falling Solder." He said that he took the photo while in the trenches. Soldiers would rush off in groups to charge at the opposing side. During one of the charges, Capa held up his camera and took this famous photo.

"The Falling Soldier" by Robert Capa

photojournalist (foh-toh-JUR-nuh-list): a photographer who takes photographs of news events and tells the story of what has happened through the photos

Capa continued working as a photojournalist during WWII. One event that led to more of Capa's most famous photographs was the Allied invasion of German-occupied France, also known as D-Day. D-Day was one of the largest invasions by sea in history. Capa was right there with the soldiers. This was a risky thing for him to do.

Mines buried along the beach were blowing up as unknowing soldiers stepped on them. Capa was surrounded by bullets flying in every direction. Ignoring these dangers, he took as many pictures as he could during his 90 minutes on the beach. Then, he ran to safety. The images Capa took during the landing gave the public then and now an incredible look at the historic day.

Robert Capa

Capa was right in the middle of the fighting on D-Day, where he took some of his most famous photographs.

Sha Fei

Sha Fei was an important Chinese photojournalist who captured iconic images of the Second Sino-Japanese War in 1937. He was on the front lines with the Chinese troops and took memorable pictures of the fighting atop the Great Wall. These images, like many of Sha Fei's photos, served as **propaganda**, providing the people with a symbol of national resistance.

propaganda (prah-puh-GAN-duh): information that is spread to influence the way people think, to gain supporters, or to damage an opposing group. It is often, but not always, biased information

Sha Fei

Fighting took place right atop the Great Wall during the Second Sino-Japanese War.

It is always dangerous to be a photojournalist in combat. In one instance, Sha Fei was wounded during an attack, leaving his film unprotected. The soldiers knew how important his work was. Nine of them were killed while trying to protect Sha Fei's film.

Sha Fei died at 38, but he is remembered as a war photojournalist with great empathy and artistic talent. He had the ability to draw true emotion out of his subjects.

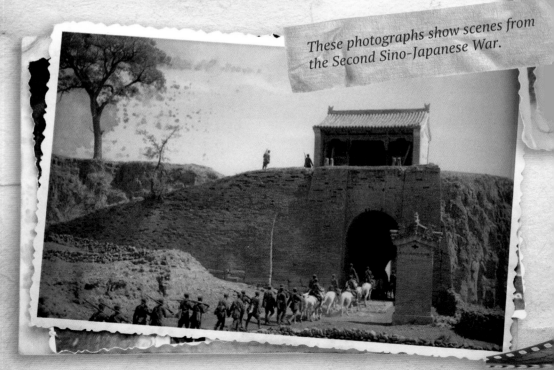

These photographs show scenes from the Second Sino-Japanese War.

Catherine Leroy

Catherine Leroy was a photojournalist known for her bravery. She started reporting on the Vietnam War in 1966. She worked as a freelancer and would sell her pictures after she took them. Because she wasn't on assignment from a publication, she didn't have much money. To save money, Leroy lived among the troops, eating what they ate and sleeping where they slept.

Catherine Leroy

A photograph by Catherine Leroy of a group of U.S. Marines in Vietnam.

Leroy got her parachutist license when she was a teenager. This skill proved helpful during the war. She parachuted with the troops during Operation Junction City. She was the first ever journalist to parachute jump into combat, and she took pictures of the troops in midair.

Leroy in parachute gear before her jump.

Leroy took photos of troops in midair during her jump.

During the war, Leroy was captured by the North Vietnamese Army. A French journalist was captured alongside her. One lieutenant was able to speak French. They were able to explain to the lieutenant that they were journalists and not soldiers. The lieutenant agreed to let them go.

Leroy is given a pin to commemorate the historic moment of being the first journalist to parachute jump into combat.

First, Leroy persuaded her captors to allow her to photograph them. She told them she wanted to show their side of the story. The photographs of these men were published in *Life* magazine. Leroy wrote the article to go along with the images she took.

Leroy won the George Polk Award for Picture of the Year in 1967 for her work in Vietnam. She is remembered as one of the greatest photojournalists of the Vietnam War.

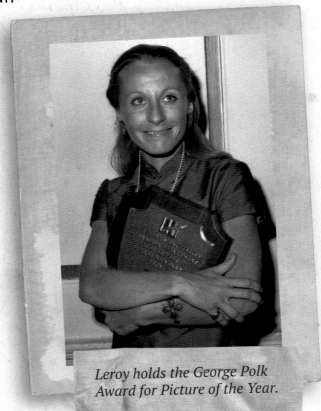

Leroy holds the George Polk Award for Picture of the Year.

Leroy captured images of troops in Vietnam while she traveled with them.

Memory Game

Look at the pictures. What do you remember reading on the pages where each image appeared?

Index

After-Reading Questions

1. What did Basil Clarke change about war reporting?

2. Why did Roi Ottley have to soften the reality he saw between Black and white soldiers in his reports?

3. What was the name of the image that made Robert Capa famous?

4. What was the location of some of Sha Fei's most memorable war photos?

5. Catherine Leroy was the first reporter to do what?

Activity

Imagine you are going to interview one of the journalists from this book. Write a list of questions for your subject. Using the library or the internet, try to find the answers to your questions.

About the Author

Allen R. Wells loved researching and refamiliarizing himself with the hidden figures in this book. Allen admires their perseverance and determination to fight for what they believe. He writes wherever he finds inspiration. He lives in Atlanta, Georgia, where he works as a mechanical engineer and children's author.

www.rourkeeducationalmedia.com

PHOTO CREDITS: cover: eastern archive/ Shutterstock.com, LiliGraphie/ Shutterstock.com, jannoon028/ Shutterstock.com, Juan Pablo Olaya Celis / Shutterstock.com, FabrikaSimf/ Shutterstock.com; Inside Cover: DarkBird/ Shutterstock.com, jannoon028/ Shutterstock.com, Juan Pablo Olaya Celis / Shutterstock.com; TOC: waku/ Shutterstock.com; TOC, page 32: TADDEUS/ Shutterstock.com; page 4-5, 6-7, 14-15, 26-27, 28-29: DarkBird/ Shutterstock.com; page 4, 8, 12, 16, 20, 24: DarkBird/ Shutterstock.com; page 5, 7, 9, 13, 17, 19, 21, 22, 25, 26, 27, 28, 29: Picsfive/ Shutterstock.com; page 5: fozrocket/ Getty Images, jannoon028/ Shutterstock.com; page 6: vladee/ Shutterstock.com; page 7: Everett Collection/ Shutterstock.com, azure1/ Shutterstock.com; page 8: casa.da.photo/ Shutterstock.com; page 8 ,12, 16: LiliGraphie/ Shutterstock.com ; page 9: Popartic/ Shutterstock.com, U.S. Holocaust Museum, Nataliia K/ Shutterstock.com, Katrien1/ Shutterstock.com; page 9, 30: Wikimedia Commons; page 10-11, 20-21: DarkBird/ Shutterstock.com; page 11: spatuletail / Shutterstock.com, Everett Collection/ Shutterstock.com, Vitaly Korovin/ Shutterstock.com; page 12-13, 22-23, 30-31: sozon/ Shutterstock.com; page 13: Kaspars Grinvalds/ Shutterstock.com; page 13, 30: Black Past; page 14: raclro/ Getty Images; page 15: Associated Press, Krasovski Dmitri/ Shutterstock.com, Assoicated Press, Krasovski Dmitri/ Shutterstock.com, Photo Win1/ Shutterstock.com, Mark Carrel/ Shutterstock.com; page 16-17: photonova/ Shutterstock.com; page 16: Versanna/ Shutterstock.com; page 17: Robert Capa © International Center of Photography; page 18-19: Olga_Z/Getty Images; page 18: Versanna/ Shutterstock.com; page 19: Robert Capa © International Center of Photography; page 19, 30: Wikimedia Commons; page 21: Juan Pablo Olaya Celis / Shutterstock.com; page 21, 30: Wikimedia Commons; page 22: Wikimedia Commons, Vitaly Korovin/ Shutterstock.com; page 22-23: SVK16/ Shutterstock.com; page 23: Wikimedia Commons, photka/ Shutterstock.com; page 24: Strela Studio/ Shutterstock.com; page 25: Associated Press, Andrey_Kuzmin/ Shutterstock.com, AP Photo/Catherine Leroy, page 26, 30: Associated Press; page 26: azure1/ Shutterstock.com, © Dotation Catherine Leroy; page 27: Associated Press, azure1/ Shutterstock.com, page 28: Assoicated Press, Strela Studio/ Shutterstock.com; page 29: © Fondation Gilles Caron, © Dotation Catherine Leroy;

Edited by: Hailey Scragg
Cover and interior design by: Morgan Burnside

Library of Congress PCN Data

Journalists / Allen R. Wells
(Beyond the Battlefield)
  ISBN 978-1-73164-901-0 (hard cover)
  ISBN 978-1-73164-849-5 (soft cover)
  ISBN 978-173164-953-9 (e-Book)
  ISBN 978-173165-005-4 (ePub)
Library of Congress Control Number: 2021935277

Rourke Educational Media
Printed in the United States of America
01-1872111937